The Gamer's Bible Study
Brant D. Baker

A creative project of Catalyst@fpc

Gray Baker
Dustin DeLong
Katie Fenwick
Kara Gregory
Amberly Huizar
Jordan Jekel
Tyler Post
Todd Ramsey
Tricia Ramsey
and a few of our friends

The Gamer's Bible Study
Copyright @ 2013 by Brant D. Baker

ISBN-13: 978-1495400759
ISBN-10: 1495400751

All scripture is taken from the New Revised Standard Version of the Bible unless otherwise noted.

The Gamer's Bible Study

~one~
THE QUEST

~two~
OVER POWERED

~three~
WHO ARE YOU?

~four~
MINERAL MANAGEMENT

~five~
GOOD VS EVIL

~six~
RULES AND CHEATS

~one~
THE QUEST

> **DISCUSS:**
>
> Why do some people like gaming? What is the attraction?
>
> What is the highest level you have achieved in any game?
>
> What is your favorite game involving a quest and why?

READ:

For a gamer the initial attraction to a new game is often figuring out how to run the game as fast as possible. It's a skills challenge, pure and simple.

But in some of the games (especially MMORPGs) there is progress and development that happens as your character sets off on a *quest*. This is especially the case in role-playing games (RPGs), where rewards can include new skills, abilities, in-game

---

Game speak:

MMOs – Massive Multiplayer Online games. These games are played online (as opposed to board or card games) across all continents, sometimes by millions of players.

MMORPGs – MMOs that are also Role Playing Games, in which the player takes on the identity of a character in the game.

World of Warcraft – perhaps THE most popular MMORPG that uses questing as a primary game mechanic.

NPC – non-playing character (a character who is not part of the MMORPG but is simply part of the game)

currency, access to new locations or weapons, or any combination of these. Quests can also be used to provide players with more background on the location or storyline of the game.

In its most basic form a quest involves a set of instructions leading to a goal, or provides clues to problems that need to be solved. Quests are common in storytelling generally, and the "epic quest" in particular had great importance in medieval literature as a search for something of greater and deeper meaning (think of the quest for the Holy Grail) ("The Quest Problem in Computer Games," Susana Tosca, www.it-c.dk/people/tosca/quest.htm).

As a game mechanic questing is used to break up the primary repetitive action of the game (for example, killing creatures). Some quests take only a few minutes to complete, while others can take hours or even days. Usually the bigger the prize the longer it will take for the quest, not to mention needing to meet certain pre-conditions before even getting started.

There are a handful of quest types, although sometimes they are bundled together.

- A "kill quest," as the name suggests, sends the character out to kill a specific number creatures. These types of quests often require the character to bring back proof of their work, such as boar tusks, wolf pelts, and so forth.

- The "combo quest" requires a player to attack certain enemies or structures with a combination of attacks until the required number of combos has reached. Enemies in these quests are usually either immortal or infinite in number.

- A "delivery quest," sometimes called a FedEx quest, involves the player being sent, as the name implies, to deliver an item from one location to another. Sometimes the character needs to first collect the item, and/or go through unfamiliar or dangerous terrain, and/or face a time limit.

- The "gather quest" requires a character to collect a number of items. Sometimes these items can be gathered from a location, sometimes they require the player to kill creatures in order to collect the required items. One variation of this quest requires the character to assemble the items into some kind of device.

- The "escort quest" is a combination of killing monsters to maintain the well-being of an NPC, while at the same time exploring a location with them. Escort quests are a particularly useful game mechanic to force players into new geographies in order to play out a scene or reveal a section of the plot (wikipedia.org/wiki/Quest_(video_gaming))

- A "puzzle quest" requires solving a kind of special challenge, the rearrangement of various shapes into the "solution" shape

- Finally, some older games had "unknown quests" where the character had to try to figure out what do: something needed to be done, and the quest entailed both figuring out what it was and how to do it!

> **Discuss:**
> What is your favorite type of quest and why?

READ:

"Life is a journey, not a destination." Although this quote is often attributed to Ralph Waldo Emerson, the actual phrase comes from a minister named Lynn H. Hough, in a 1920 Sunday School Lesson about Simon Peter. Hough may have picked up on the idea from a 1854 article that offered the advice "You should learn in early youth that your life is a journey, not a rest" (quoteinvestigator.com/2012/08/31/life-journey/)

> **Discuss:**
>
> Do you agree or disagree with the idea of life being a journey? Why or why not?

READ:

It's probably not an accident that the these thoughts come from religious sources. It turns out that the Bible is full of examples of faith journeys or "quests"

In Genesis 12 God tells Abram, "<u>GO</u> from your country and your kindred and your father's house to the land that I will show you. I will make of you a great nation, and I will bless you, and make your name great, so that you will be a blessing (v 1-2). In this quest Abram is tested in ways he never imagined, and in the end is transformed into Abraham, the father of the nation of Israel.

In Exodus God tells Moses, "I will <u>SEND</u> you to Pharaoh to <u>BRING</u> my people, the Israelites, out of Egypt" (v 10). In this quest Moses the runaway criminal (he had killed a man and so had to get out of town) is transformed into a man who is deliverer, law giver, and prophet.

In 1 Samual 17 the young shepherd boy David goes to visit his brothers on the front lines of a war that is being fought against the Philistines. The Philistines have a gigantic hero fighting for them, a big dude named Goliath, and all of the Israelites are afraid of him. David (who was probably 12-13 years old at the time), said he would go fight him, to which King Saul says, "<u>GO</u>, and may the Lord be with you" (v 37). In this quest David goes from being shepherd boy to military leader, and from there goes on to become the greatest king of Israel.

In Matthew 28 Jesus tells his followers, "All authority in heaven and on earth has been given to me. <u>GO</u> therefore and make disciples of all nations, baptizing them in the name of the Father and of the Son and of the Holy Spirit, and teaching them to obey everything that I have commanded you. And remember, I am with you always, to the end of the age" (18-20). In this quest all those who follow Jesus are invited to share the gift they have received, to keep telling other people that we are loved by God, that our sins are forgiven in his cross, and that we are now therefore free to love and forgive others.

In Philippians 3:13b-14 we find these words written by the Apostle Paul: "...forgetting what lies behind and straining forward to what lies ahead, I <u>PRESS ON</u> toward the goal for the prize of the heavenly call of God in Christ Jesus." In *The Message* these same verses say, "I've got my eye on the goal, where God is beckoning us onward—to Jesus. I'm off and running, and I'm not turning back."

It seems that our life as Christians is "a journey not a destination." When it comes to our faith God doesn't intend for us to stand still. Growing, learning, and being challenged to go on different "God quests" are all part of the adventure God has in store for us.

> **DISCUSS:**
>
> Describe a God quest you are on right now, OR a God quest you have been on, OR a God quest you think might be in your future.
>
> What does this quest look like day to day in

WRITE:

What was your key insight from this study, and what do you personally need to do about it?

~two~
"Over Powered"

> **DISCUSS:**
>
> What is your favorite game that uses *mana* and why?
>
> What do you know about the origin of *mana* as a gaming term?

READ:

Contrary to what some might thing, gaming *mana* is not the same as *manna* in the Bible. In the Old Testament God provided *manna* to the Israelites as they made their escape from Pharaoh (Exodus 16).

> In the popular card game **Magic: The Gathering**, *mana* is used to cast spells and summon creatures. It comes in different colors that are generated by a different type of land (white *mana* from Plains, blue from Islands, black from Swamps, red from Moun-tains, green from Forests).

The word itself comes from a play on words in Hebrew: when the Israelites first saw it they asked, "What is it?" which in Hebrew is *man hu.* The Bible says that this "bread from heaven" was "like coriander seed, white, and the taste of it was like wafers made with honey" (Exodus 16:31. It is worth noting that the *manna* didn't last through the night, meaning that the Israelites had to be reliant

> game speak:
>
> **qq** - quit complaining
>
> **gg** – good game
>
> **noob** – new player (but usually used in a derogatory way about someone who is a bad player)
>
> **OOM** – out of mana
>
> **op** – over-powered
>
> **IRL** – in real life

on God's faithfulness each and every day to provide their "daily bread" once more.

In the gaming world the origin of *mana* seems traceable to fantasy writer Larry Niven, who in a short story written in 1969 described *mana* as a kind of natural resource used by wizards to cast magic spells. He later expanded on this idea, developing a kind of economic model of *mana* as a limited resource which would eventually led to the end of all magic when *mana* is depleted.

Other types or uses of *mana* can be found in Polynesian culture where *mana* is a sacred impersonal force that exists in the universe. To have *mana* is to have influence, power, and authority. *Mana* can come to a person through birth or through combat.

In Hawaiian culture the spiritual energy of *mana* can also take on healing properties, and can be found not only in people but also in objects and places (and so, for example, the island of Molokai was thought to possess strong *mana* and so many battles were fought to gain control over it). It is the Hawaiian belief that every action carries with it the chance to gain or lose *mana* (wikipedia.org/mana).

> **DISCUSS:**
>
> In what ways does the concept of *mana* work in real life? Does it describe any scientific or spiritual reality that you are personally familiar with?

READ:

The spiritual power available to Christians is the Holy Spirit. Just before his ascension Jesus tells his followers that they will receive "power" from on high, so that they can spread the word about Jesus to the ends of the earth (Acts 1:8). The word "power" comes from a Greek word "dunamis" which can also mean energy, might, or great force (it is the root word for "dynamite" in English!).

Earlier Jesus had told Nicodemus "the wind blows where it chooses, and you hear the sound of it, but you do not know where it comes from or where it goes. So it is with everyone who is born of the Spirit" (John 3:8). Among other things the implication here seems to be that we don't have the ability to control the Holy Spirit.

> **DISCUSS:**
>
> How is it a good thing that people are not able to control things by the use of magic? Give examples of things that could go terribly wrong if individual people really had that kind of power.
>
> How is the power of the Holy Spirit different from *mana*?

READ:

The Bible talks about believers in Jesus having the fruit of the Spirit: love, joy, peace, forbearance, kindness, goodness, faithfulness, gentleness and self-control (Galatians 5:22-23). Of these, which ones are OP in your life, and in which are you OOM?

Remember: you are OP IRL thanks to the Holy Spirit!

WRITE:

What was your key insight from this study, and what do you personally need to do about it?

~three~
"Who Are You?"

> **DISCUSS:**
> Who is your favorite game character to play?

READ:

In **RPGs** (role playing games) such as *World of Warcraft, Runescape, Final Fantasy,* and *Banjo Kazooie* (just to name a few) a player is asked to create or become a character. In addition to race, class, and gender, characters usually have certain attributes, strengths, and weaknesses. These attributes are typically given a numerical value. For example, on a 10 point scale a character may have an initial strength (or power) of 5, ability (or skill) of 7, and stamina (or endurance) of 3. These values can increase or decrease with developments in the game, such as engaging in a battle, which may leave the character momentarily weaker, but upon recovery having a higher skill level.

In many computer games, especially FPSs (first-person shooters), the player character lacks a unique (or

---

game speak:

skin – a term derived from the computer generated "mesh" used by game developers to cloth a character. It is more broadly used to describe either a character's outfit or appearance. Often the same character comes with a number of "skins" for players to choose.

FPS - First person shooters, games in which the player is primarily involved in killing: the player "sees" through the eyes of the character (as opposed to seeing their character move through the game on-screen)

pk – player killer: in RPGs a player kills creatures, but in some RPGs a player can also kill other players. Someone who does this is called a **pk**. Don't be a pk!

known) identity. In these games the character has no name and engages in no dialogue. Other non-player characters will typically address the player as though they don't expect a verbal response. Intriguingly, such games are also known for lacking mirrors that a player can look into and see their own reflection (Wikipedia.org/wiki/Player_character).

> **DISCUSS:**
>
> Why do you pick the character you do? What factors into your decision to play as one character over another?

READ:

We all carry a variety of roles or identities.

Some people are defined by their <u>work</u>. They say "I'm a plumber," or "I'm an accountant," or "I'm a nurse." The problem, of course, is that if you are unemployed or retired, your "identity" suddenly disappears.

Some people are defined by their abilities. They say "I'm an athlete," or "I'm a model," or even "I'm a gamer." The danger here, of course, is that some abilities don't last—we grow old, our looks fade, we lose our internet connection (!) and then what do we do?

Still other people are defined by their behaviors. They say, "I'm an alcoholic," or "I'm a homosexual," or "I'm a loser." Many of us have labels that we've carried with us throughout our life and we let those behaviors and labels define who we are.

The Bible says that "if anyone is in Christ, there is a new creation: everything old has passed away; see, everything has become new! All this is from God, who reconciled us to himself through Christ, and has given us the ministry of reconciliation; that is, in Christ God was reconciling the world to himself, not counting their trespasses against them, and entrusting the message of reconciliation to us" (2 Corinthians 5:17-19).

Here are a couple more "child of God" verses:

- "But to all who received him, who believed in his name, he gave power to become children of God..." (John 1:12)

- "For all who are led by the Spirit of God are children of God" (Romans 8:14)

- And because you are children, God has sent the Spirit of his Son into our hearts, crying, "Abba! Father!" (Galatians 4:6)

- "See what love the Father has given us, that we should be called children of God; and that is what we are" (1 John 3:1)

WRITE:

Copy the verse that speaks to you most about your identity as a child of God.

Our true identity, the only one that matters, is what God sees. No matter what we do for a living, no matter what abilities we might have, no matter even what good or bad behaviors there are in our life, as Christians who we are is defined by the sacrifice of Jesus Christ who has made us children of God.

What is really going on here is a variation of the whole "who's your daddy?" question. If your dad was a farmer or a mechanic you might think of yourself in one way—his identity (defined by his work) might inform your own. But if your dad was the president, or a king, then your identity might be very different indeed! What the Bible says is that your dad is God...any questions?!

> **DISCUSS:**
>
> What does it mean to you that you are a child of God? How does it change how you see yourself?
>
> Share with the group which of the verses above about being children of God speaks to you the most, and then write it in the space below. Consider memorizing it this week.

READ:

In the gaming world "spawning" is the creation of a character, and "re-spawning" is the recreation of character after death or destruction. Essentially the character gets another life. The Christian way to look at this is that we are re-spawned in Christ, we are born again, resurrected into a whole new character called "Child of God." How cool is that?

WRITE:

What was your key insight from this study, and what do you personally need to do about it?

HOT BUTTON

What issues <u>might</u> there be for a Christian in playing a first person shooter game?

~four~
"Mineral Management"

> **DISCUSS:**
> What is your favorite resource management game and why?

READ:

"IN THE DISTANT FUTURE, THE NEWLY FORMED *TERRAN DOMINION* FACES THE ARRIVAL OF TWO HOSTILE ALIEN RACES: THE SAVAGE *ZERG* AND THE ENIGMATIC *PROTOSS*. GATHER RESOURCES AND EXPAND YOUR FORCES TO LEAD THEM TO VICTORY. THE ONLY ALLIES ARE ENEMIES. THE ONLY CHOICE IS WAR."

> Game speak:
>
> **gaming platforms** – the device or system on which a game is played. Popular gaming platforms include xBox, PS3, PC/Windows, and Wii.
>
> **game engine** – the operating code, used by game designers
>
> **game development and distribution companies** – Blizzard Entertainment (behind Starcraft and Warcraft among others), Steam (one of the largest in the world), Activision (Tony Hawk, Call of Duty), LucasArts (Star Wars), and Nintendo (Mario Bros, Donkey Kong, Pokémon, and many others).

So reads the homepage of the game StarCraft, a military science fiction strategy game. StarCraft is particularly popular in South Korea, where players and teams can participate in professional competitions and earn sponsorships.

StarCraft is one example of a game that relies heavily on *the management (or stewardship) of resources* (other examples include *Skyrim, Minecraft, and Settlers of Catan)*. Typical game resources can include such things as raw materials (or natural resources), money (or tokens or treasure or game points), energy (or strength or power), human resources, mana, land, spells, health, and even time.

In Starcraft each of the opposing races rely on two resources in particular to sustain their game economies and to build their forces. The first resource is minerals, which are obtained by using a worker unit to harvest the resource mineral nodes scattered around the battlefield. The second resource is vespene gas, which is used to construct advanced units and buildings, and is acquired by building a refinery on top of a geyser ("General Strategy: Resources" on www.Battle.net).

DISCUSS:

In your opinion what is the hardest resource to manage well IRL (in real life) and why?

READ:

In the gaming world the stewardship of resources can involve players in planning, self-preservation, spying on enemies, and even hoarding. It can also elicit teamwork as players work together to gain mutually beneficial resource prizes. Often times players will be offered an opportunity to press their luck, or seize the moment, in a risk-reward type of situation. Knowing when to take these risks versus knowing when to exercise impulse control is often the difference between defeat and victory.

In the real world the stewardship of resources relates to at least two biblical issues. The first is the concept of wisdom, and the Bible has lots to say about it. Perhaps the most succinct statement is in the book of Proverbs:

> The fear of the Lord is the beginning of knowledge;
> fools despise wisdom and instruction...
>
> Wisdom cries out in the street; in the squares she raises her voice.
>
> At the busiest corner she cries out; at the entrance of the city gates she speaks:
>
> "How long, O simple ones, will you love being simple?
> How long will scoffers delight in their scoffing and fools hate knowledge?
>
> Give heed to my reproof; I will pour out my thoughts to you; I will make my words known to you.
>
> Because I have called and you refused,
> have stretched out my hand and no one heeded,
> and because you have ignored all my counsel and
> would have none of my reproof,
>
> I also will laugh at your calamity; I will mock when panic strikes you, when panic strikes you like a storm, and your calamity comes like a whirlwind, when distress and anguish come upon you.
>
> Then they will call upon me, but I will not answer;
> they will seek me diligently, but will not find me...
> therefore they shall eat the fruit of their way
> and be sated with their own devices.
>
> For waywardness kills the simple, and the complacency of fools destroys them; but those who listen to me will be secure and will live at ease, without dread of disaster." (Proverbs 1:7, 20-33)

> **DISCUSS:**
>
> What words or phrases strike you the most about these verses from Proverbs?

The main message that we get from the Bible about wisdom is that it has to do with respecting God ("the fear of the Lord") and following God's commandments. Beyond these really good ideas other things at work in the definition include discipline, impulse control, and planning ahead (which are all part of resource management as well).

> **DISCUSS:**
>
> On a scale from 1 (reckless) to 10 (wise), rank the following actions
>
> - Going to the store and making an "impulse purchase"
> - Ignoring the alarm clock and sleeping "just a little while longer"
> - Setting up, <u>and following</u>, a written budget
> - Eating junk food
> - Exercising
> - Taking drugs or drinking alcohol
> - Getting homework done ahead of time
> - Hooking up with a stranger at a party or bar
> - Reading the Bible

The second biblical issue that relates to resource management is what Christians call "stewardship," which has to do with at least three things: stewardship (or management) of our talent, treasure, and time.

Talent

To one he gave five talents, to another two, to another one, to each according to his ability." (Matthew 25:15) *"Each one should use whatever gift you have received to serve others..."* (1 Peter 4:10)

What are your talents, your spiritual gifts? There's no doubt that you have at least one because the Bible is clear that God has gifted everyone in some unique way. Chances are you already have some understanding of the things that come naturally for you or that you like to do, and things that are difficult for you or that you don't like to do. The real issue here is to identify your passions, the things that are life-giving, soul-feeding, and joy-refreshing for you, and then using those in some way to serve other people.

Treasure

Bring the full tithes into the storehouse, that there may be food in my house: and thereby put me to the test, says the Lord of hosts, if I will not open the windows of heaven for you and pour down for you an overflowing blessing. (Malachi 3:10)

A *tithe* was originally the practice of bringing the first part of the harvest to the temple (see Deuteronomy 26:1-11). In this respect tithing is an act of faith. God is saying, "Trust Me to give you what you need to survive." In later times a "tithe" came to mean giving ten percent of all God has given us back to God's work, either through the church, a charitable organization, or just giving it away to someone in need.

Time

A thousand years in your sight are like yesterday when it is past, or like a watch in the night. We are like grass that is renewed in the morning and in the evening fades and withers. So teach us to count our days that we may gain a wise heart. (Selections from Psalm 90)

Time is one of the greatest resources at our disposal. We only have so much time on earth to accomplish God's will, so it's important that we don't waste it going after things that don't matter.

So how could we go about providing for God's work through a *tithe* on our time? If we were to accept the challenge to return 10% of our time to God as an act of thanksgiving, what exactly would that mean?

As a kind of mind game, let's agree that of the 168 hours a week we're all given, that God doesn't count the time we spend sleeping (56 hours) and working (say 42 hours). That leaves 70 hours a week of time that is ours to use as we please, and a tithe on that would be 7 hours a week.

Seven hours a week to return in thanksgiving to God. Let's continue our mind game and agree that we could use some of this time to worship God (say, 1.5 hours per week), some to have a daily time of reading the Bible and praying (maybe 15 minutes per day, so 2 hours per week), and some time to be involved in a youth group or Sunday School class (maybe 1.5 hours a week), all of which comes to total 5 hours. That leaves a minimum of two more hours each week to volunteer for the Kingdom of God.

> **DISCUSS:**
> How will you use those two hours to serve God each week?

WRITE:
What was your key insight from this study, and what do you personally need to do about it?

~five~
"Good vs Evil"

> **DISCUSS:**
> Why does Bowswer always lose to Mario?

READ:

Go to the simple website "Good-v-evil.com" and you'll be offered a chance to vote for one or the other. Once you vote you will see which side is winning!

John Scott Tynes, former Lead Designer at Microsoft Game Studios suggests that such simple alternatives aren't really asking for much. Games that offer this kind of decision, says Tynes, are really offering "the choice between humanity and psychopathy - will you choose to be a human being or a murderous thug? That's not a dilemma. That's the difference between function-ning and nonfunctioning brain chemistry." Tynes continues,

> In our civilization, choosing between good and evil is no dilemma. The choices we make have more to do with things like selfishness versus

---

Game speak:

Mario –a popular video game protagonist. Mario is a short, pudgy, Italian plumber who lives in the Mushroom Kingdom, where for some reason a plumber is needed to save Princess Peach, who is repeatedly kidnapped by various villains, including **Bowser,** Donkey Kong and Wario.

Game designer-what, you think these things just happen?? No, someone has to come up with the basic idea (the story), and then invent the rules and structures that will make the game work. Game designers usually oversee the work of a team that includes graphic artists, game mechanics designers, writers, programmers, environment (background) designers, and audio designers.

selflessness, determining when truth is kind and when it's cruel, and whether it's okay to cheat to achieve your goals. A real moral dilemma is truly a dilemma, not an obvious choice. It involves equally weighted good or bad outcomes.

Tynes cites none other than Luke Skywalker as an example of a character who faces a nuanced world in which small steps can lead to larger, character-shaping consequences. Most choices that he makes lack the comfort of being black and white (or dark and light, if you prefer). Instead Skywalker, like most of us, walks through a world of gray in which he can't always be sure that the outcomes of his decisions will be what he hopes or intends. His is "a long moral path" in which he needs to learn to avoid reckless decisions driven by his passions (which will eventually lead to the Dark Side) and instead make decisions and take actions that will lead to the Light (www.escapistmagazine.com).

> **DISCUSS:**
> *IRL—will good or evil triumph? Why?*

READ:
Knowing the difference between good and evil suggests a standard, and for many people across the centuries the gold standard on morality has been the ten commandments. Of course the Big Ten don't address everything, but lots of situations, however nuanced they may seem on the surface, are pretty much covered by what was on those original stone tablets.

A good way to understand the ten commandments is to phrase them in the opposite way. So, for example, "You shall not murder" becomes "You shall give life." As a group rephrase the rest:

Original > Rephrase

You shall not murder.
> *You shalt give life.*

You shall have no other gods before me.
>

You shall not make an idol
>

You shall not take the Lord's name in vain
>

Honor the sabbath day
>

Honor your father and your mother
>

You shall not commit adultery.
>

You shall not steal.
>

> ### Original > Rephrase
>
> You shall not bear false witness against your neighbor.
> >
>
> You shall not covet your neighbor's stuff.
> >

READ:

The Bible teaches us that a cosmic battle is raging all around us, a battle that we never see. A fascinating story about this is in Daniel 10. Daniel tells us that he had been in mourning for three weeks. On the 24th day he had a powerful and disturbing vision that left him weak and in a trance, flat on the ground. While he was down an angel spoke to him and let him know that God had heard him from the very first day, and that God sent the angel to comfort Daniel. "But," said the angel, "the prince of the kingdom of Persia opposed me twenty-one days. So Michael, one of the chief princes, came to help me, and I left him there with the prince of the kingdom of Persia" (Daniel 10:13). The angel goes on to comfort and encourage Daniel, but then says "Now I must return to fight against the prince of Persia, and when I am through with him, the prince of Greece will come..." (10:21). All of these "princes" are understood in context to be dark angels or demons, and what is so fascinating about this passage is the suggestion that the angels are having to duke it out with the demons when they are on their way to help us!

> **DISCUSS:**
> *How might this story help you understand the things that happen to you and the people around you? What evidence do you see of a "cosmic battle" going on?*

READ:

<u>THE</u> prime Bible passage for talking about good versus evil, angels versus demons, light versus dark is Ephesians 6. It's a kind of funny thing: anybody who has been around the church growing up probably heard about the *second* part of this passage. It is the "armor of God" passage and it says,

> *Therefore take up the whole armor of God, so that you may be able to withstand on that evil day, and having done everything, to stand firm. Stand therefore, and fasten the belt of truth around your waist, and put on the breastplate of righteousness. As shoes for your feet put on whatever will make you ready to proclaim the gospel of peace. With all of these, take the shield of faith, with which you will be able to quench all the flaming arrows of the evil one. Take the helmet of salvation, and the sword of the Spirit, which is the word of God* (Ephesians 6:13-17).

What a lot of people haven't heard is why there is a *therefore* at the start of this. Remember, you always have to ask what the "therefore" is there for! Why do we need to have all this defensive gear (note that the only weapon we have is the "sword of the Spirit," which is the Bible). Well, here's what the previous verses say:

> *Put on the whole armor of God, <u>so that</u> you may be able to stand against the wiles of the devil. For our struggle is not against enemies of blood and flesh, but against the rulers, against the authorities, against the cosmic powers of this present darkness, against the spiritual forces of evil in the heavenly places.* (Ephesians 6:11-12)

We need all that armor because we have an Ancient Enemy whose only agenda is to mess with the things God loves. And since God loves all of us, Satan wants to do everything possible to attack us. We need to be ready, suited up, and understand that those attacks are going to come, perhaps most especially the harder we try to do what is right and pleasing to God. In other words, how can you know you are living the kind of life God wants you to live? Because if you are Satan will be attacking!

> **DISCUSS:**
> *Of the various pieces of armor mentioned in Ephesians 6 -- the belt of truth, the breastplate of righteousness, shoes to proclaim the gospel of peace, and the shield of faith—which one do you think is the strongest in your life and which one is the weakest? What can you do to make the weak part strong?*

WRITE:

What was your key insight from this study, and what do you personally need to do about it?

HOT BUTTON

Is it ever acceptable for Christans to play "dark side" characters?

~six~
"Rules and Cheats"

> **DISCUSS:**
>
> *Why would a gamer want to cheat a game? If you've done so, what game do you like to cheat, and why?*

READ:

So when is it cheating and when is it just getting guidance or advice? When is it a hack and when is it just a shortcut that doesn't matter? When is it being clever and when is it being dishonest?

Perhaps we can agree that anything which is used to make a game do something it wasn't intended to do, and/or which gives an unfair advantage, is a "cheat."

Several companies have made a business out of providing cheats to frustrated gamers. Some of them, like GameShark offer other physical products for various gaming systems. Players can load cheat codes from disks

---

Game speak:

Cheats–sometimes cheats are glitches or imperfections in the original game, sometimes they come from code that is added later by players

hacking–basically the same thing as cheating

BELIEVE IT OR NOT, THERE'S AN APP FOR THAT! "Struggling with your favorite video games? Never fear--help is available. With the Game Cheats app on your Android device, you'll never have to leave your sofa to look up a cheat again."

DID THEY REALLY SAY THAT? Found on the CheatCodes.com website: "CheatCodes.com guarantees the most complete database of cheat codes anywhere...*Millions of gamers around the world have trusted us since 1996. You can trust us, too.*"

provided by these companies and then apply the cheats they are after during play.

Not surprisingly the gaming industry has responded, especially in the world of MMOs. Apparently it's one thing if you want to cheat at a game in the privacy of your own home, but it's entirely more serious if you want to cheat while playing a million online opponents! The most significant of these countermeasures come from *Hackshield,* "developed by a Korean security solutions company.

> DISCUSS:
>
> *Can an argument be made that finding an d using cheats is actually part of the game, maybe "the game within the game?"*

READ:

Wiki defines cheating like this, "an immoral way of achieving a goal...breaking of rules to gain unfair advantage in a competitive situation...the getting of reward for ability by dishonest means. This broad definition will necessarily include acts of bribery, cronyism, sleaze, nepotism and any situation where individuals are given preference using inappropriate criteria" (/Cheating).

On many moral issues the world tends to say, "As long as nobody gets hurt then it's ok..." The problem is that it's usually very easy for the one who is about to benefit to be convinced that their action isn't going to cause harm. Personal benefit tends to obscure public awareness!

The Bible, on the other hand, says "You shall not cheat in measuring length, weight, or quantity. You shall not cheat one another, but you shall fear your God; for I am the Lord your God" (Leviticus 19:35 & 25:17).

> **DISCUSS:**
>
> *Sometimes gamers use cheats simply to have more fun, either by winning faster or by "maxing out" the game. Is there really any harm in this?*

READ:

If the Bible had a Rule Book it might be the Ten Commandments (see Lesson 5). But as Christians we are actually called to an even higher standard. A big section of the Sermon on the Mount has Jesus telling his followers that he has come to "fulfill" the law, that is, to fill it full of life and meaning. He then goes on to offer a series of "you have heard it said...but I say to you..." teachings that have rocked the world ever since.

"You have heard that it was said to those of ancient times, 'You shall not murder'; and 'whoever murders shall be liable to judgment.' **But I say to you** that if you are angry with a brother or sister, you will be liable to judgment; and if you insult a brother or sister, you will be liable to the council; and if you say, 'You fool,' you will be liable to the hell of fire. So when you are offering your gift at the altar, if you remember that your brother or sister has something against you, leave your gift there before the altar and go; first be reconciled to your brother or sister, and then come and offer your gift. Come to terms quickly with your accuser while you are on the way to court with him, or your accuser may hand you over to the judge, and the judge to the guard, and you will be thrown into prison. Truly I tell you, you will never get out until you have paid the last penny.

"**You have heard that it was said**, 'You shall not commit adultery.' **But I say to you** that everyone who looks at a woman with lust has already committed adultery with her in his heart. If your right eye causes you to sin, tear it out and throw it away; it is better for you to lose one of your members than for your whole body to be thrown into hell. And if your right hand causes you to sin, cut it off and throw it away; it is better for you to lose one of your members than for your whole body to go into hell.

"**It was also said**, 'Whoever divorces his wife, let him give her a certificate of divorce.' **But I say to you** that anyone who divorces his wife, except on the ground of unchastity, causes her to commit adultery; and whoever marries a divorced woman commits adultery.

"Again, **you have heard that it was said** to those of ancient times, 'You shall not swear falsely, but carry out the vows you have made to the Lord.' **But I say to you**, Do not swear at all, either by heaven, for it is the throne of God, or by the earth, for it is his footstool, or by Jerusalem, for it is the city of the great King. And do not swear by your head, for you cannot make one hair white or black. Let your word be 'Yes, Yes' or 'No, No'; anything more than this comes from the evil one.

"**You have heard that it was said**, 'An eye for an eye and a tooth for a tooth.' **But I say to you**, Do not resist an evildoer. But if anyone strikes you on the right cheek, turn the other also; and if anyone wants to sue you and take your coat, give your cloak as well; and if anyone forces you to go one mile, go also the second mile. Give to everyone who begs from you, and do not refuse anyone who wants to borrow from you.

"**You have heard that it was said**, 'You shall love your neighbor and hate your enemy.' **But I say to you**, Love your enemies and pray for those who persecute you, so that you may be children of your Father in heaven; for he makes his sun rise on the evil and on the good, and sends rain on the righteous and on the unrighteous. For if you love those who love you, what reward do you have? Do not even the tax collectors do the same? And if you greet only your brothers and sisters, what more are you doing than others? Do not even the Gentiles do the same? Be perfect, therefore, as your heavenly Father is perfect" (Matthew 5:21-48).

> **DISCUSS:**
> Which of these "fulfilling rules of life" is the hardest, which is the easiest, and why?
> Not all of these situations apply to every life, and not all of life is covered by these teachings. Looking at your own life, what one "fulfilling" thing do you plan to work on this week?

WRITE:

What was your key insight from this study, and what do you personally need to do about it?

Printed in Great Britain
by Amazon.co.uk, Ltd.,
Marston Gate.